Back To Grace

Spiritual poetry and reflections

Earthschool Harmony

Back To Grace

First published 2014

A copy of this publication can be found in the
National Library of Australia.

ISBN: 978-0-6484472-0-7 (pbk.) 978-0-6484472-1-4 (ebook)

Published by Earthschool Harmony

A poet is someone who can pour light
into a cup, then raise it to nourish your
beautiful parched, holy mouth.
~ Hafiz

Contents

This book is dedicated to Kai, Zali and Maya Nova who gave my heart wings.

Back to Grace

From the veil of darkness
consumed
by spiritual hunger
I began
my holy pilgrimage
back to grace

Ecstatic Rapture

Sacred chants of worship
spiral up into the light
dancing from the lips
of a soul
in ecstatic rapture

The intense pulse
of devotional prayer
enfolds me like a holy cloak
and permeates
my being

Within this sacred vibration
I am bathed in purity

I am one
with the soul of the universe

Truth

To hear truth
still your mind

The eternal teacher
whispers to you
in silence

Self Love

Your essence is love
it has forever been
your spiritual birthright

Why do you hide
behind your illusions
of imperfection
passing judgment
on yourself

Do not allow
your thinking mind
to be an obstacle
to the truth

Rest within

Surrender your pain
look within and see
your perfect and divine
self

Stardust

We came one day from stardust
to walk upon the earth
born mortal into body
but spiritual by birth

We came to earth to speak the truth
to whisper in the winds
to join the colors of the earth
the colors of our skins

For all are pure and full of grace
connected throughout time
there is no separation
for spirit is divine

So hold your face up to the sun
and listen to the winds
lift the veil that clouds your eyes
in truth
your life begins

Eyes of Reverence

As you journey through life
bringing your unique experiences
into expression
remember
in each moment
to look at what lies beneath
your earthly robe

Look with eyes of reverence
to see the holiness
of your authentic self

Metamorphosis

Out of the darkness
into the light
don't be afraid
let your wings take flight

You will be guided
along the way
angels and loved ones
are with you each day

My wish for you
is peace on earth

My blessings are with you
for your rebirth

Sounds of Silence

On the journey to find yourself
cleanse your mind
be still
infuse
with the holy vibration

Within these sounds of silence
another world awaits
where
with great tenderness
the beloved whispers to you

Life's Lessons

I often give thanks and blessings
to the things we perceive as mistakes
for I know they are life's lessons
and with each my soul awakes

Each one will come again and again
unless you choose to see
perhaps there is a different path
perception holds the key

With your heart and mind wide open
you learn a better way
Forgive yourself and be gentle
lessons learnt for one day

Like a Prayer

Each of us an artist
painting the rich texture
of another world into being
offering a visual feast
to nourish the soul

Each of us a poet
weaving words of love
into creation
a robe of celestial knowledge
to wrap around you
and illuminate your heart

Each of us a musician
singing into expression
a mystical vibration of healing
sacred sounds
to shift consciousness

These gifts are offered to you
like a prayer

Lullaby

I breathe you in
until I can no longer distinguish
that which is you
and that which is me

The veil of dualism parts
giving birth to a sacred union
of one

A mystical symphony
permeates my senses
and a holy lullaby
embraces me

Tonight I sleep
within the rapture

Illusion

Breathe in light
and surrender
to the primal source
of love

Remember seeker
our earthly perceptions
of reality
are just an illusion

Love
is who you are

Chalice of Enlightenment

Years lost in the labyrinth
of illusion and personal myth
wandering the hallways of time

Entangled in the veils
of darkness and ignorance
until ancient writings
and sacred whispers
seeped through the cracks of my soul

I drank intoxicated
from the chalice of enlightenment
each whisper ascending my spirit
further towards the light
of eternal truth

Souls Entwined

You came one day my loved one
upon a prayer into my life
with souls entwined our children born
you took me as your spiritual wife

My love has been abundant
our children are our masterpiece
two paths now one and unified
we made a home and found release

The universe has blessed me
I live my life in great delight

In turn I wish to bless you too
and pray you live
in love and light

Sweet Benediction

Seasons transform
day welcomes night
all things change

Allow the sacredness
of each moment to unfold

Do not mourn
the ghost of loss

Change
is the sweet benediction
that brings you closer
to your soul's purpose

Sacred Fire

A sacred fire burns
deep within your soul
this fire of eternal truth
connects you
to the whole

Rapture of The Mystery

As earth time
peels back another layer
the illusion of a new year begins

Some dance wild in the streets
intoxicated on wine and diversion

I sit by the light of the full moon
intoxicated by grace

An offering of a poem
spiritually conceived
is illuminated into words

I am drawn graciously
a little deeper
into the rapture of the mystery

The Invitation

Once you invite
the beloved
across the threshold
of your open heart
you sense
with pure clarity
no greater expression
of love exists
than this union
of one

Pilgrimage

All who walk the path of contemplation
in search of the divine mystery
are entangled
in the eternal vastness
of the thinking mind

Along the pilgrimage
walking the path of our spiritual quest
we leave footprints on the thinking mind
like obstacles to the truth

After many paths and many years
perhaps many lifetimes
we become aware
of the sacredness of our suffering

We return humbled
entering the doorway of our hearts
knowing the holiness
within silence
knowing love
is our elixir

Kindred Spirits

There are many kindred spirits
I call family
they have been impregnated
upon my heart
leaving footprints
upon my soul

Not all are connected
by blood
but we are forever united
with the sacred thread
of love

The Gift

Beautiful child
gift from the universe
eyes that shine wisdom
beyond words spoken

Everything will be alright
beautiful child
for you shine
in love

Earth Suits

As spiritual beings we come to earth
our earth suits chosen before our birth
The different colors that we wear
souls together
in spirit we share

We are immortal and must see
divine guidance always with thee
Do not pass judgment onto others
for all are sisters
or our brothers

In spiritual closet you cannot hide
for ignorance will divide
Blend our colors and rejoice
with souls entwined
we have one voice

Awakened

Awakened
you hear
the holy language
of silence

You see the light
of love
within the darkness

Once awakened
your illuminated soul
will never go back
to sleep

Blessed Be

May you awaken this day
to the holiness
of your own being

May you honour yourself
follow your dreams
and feel your connection
with the primordial light

May divine love
be illuminated into words
in each sacred encounter
through your day

May absolute joy
weave its way into laughter
that permeates the holy shrine
of your heart

Blessed be

Purification

Open the door
step over the threshold of illusion
and come home to the divine source
of your heart

Pull back the mystic curtain
that veils your eyes
be a seeker
of truth

Anoint with great love
and release the ties
that bind
your mortal wounds

Embrace your purification
give birth to your sacred self

Let the light in

Synthesis

Division
of divine presence
into many different names
brings with it fear and war
where no one really gains

All the different scriptures
carry messages of truth
all souls are one and sacred
let us teach this to our youth

There is just one creator
we see through different eyes
but messages of love and peace
only ignorance denies

We can bring peace on earth
transformation with intent
it takes all souls to unify
no longer to fragment

Soul Sisters

Soul sisters
I bless you my friends
joined together
love descends

A sacred circle
always aware
in body
soul
and spirit
we share

The Power of Love

Within the mists of ancient memory
through the illusion of duality
the thread of oneness
awakens in you

Your spiritual heart imbibes
in the primordial light
and
as you dance towards infinity
you begin to see
all things are held together
by the power of love

Reflection

Some days
you may look into the mirror
and not recognise yourself
but I see you
I know who you are

You are child of the universe
a free spirit

You are love
expressing itself
in its many different forms

You are not lost
you are on a pilgrimage
experiencing all that there is
in this earthly form

You are never alone

Go gently on yourself
you are safe and loved
you are welcomed and cherished

Look into that mirror
and see what I see

I see a perfect soul

And so it is

What Would Love Do Now

In every sacred moment
as you walk your pilgrimage
with each divine encounter
as soul meets soul
when you look with eyes of reverence
and see into the holiness of things
just for that moment
be still and ask yourself
what would love do now

My Essence

I can't see you
but I know you are there

I can't touch you
but I feel your presence

I can't hear you
yet you whisper into my soul

I breathe you in

You are my essence

Other Lifetimes

Deep recesses of the mind
hold glimpses of another kind
of long ago and other times
memory surfaces and reminds
us of the past and sacred days
we walked the earth
in different ways

Wisdom of the days gone by
stay with us held in mind's eye
each a lesson to recall
none too big or too small
for all are sacred and fill our hearts
as each life ends
and new lives start

May the light of truth always shine
as our mortal and spiritual lives entwine
throughout our journey along the way
may a deeper knowing
infuse each day

Songbird

Eyes open to the ecstasy of life
she dances and twirls
heart and arms wide open
feeling with her soul
all the agony and joys
her connection to all people

Raw alive and on fire
the embers of change
seep through her veins
igniting her path
erupting in the beauty
of song

Earth goddess
siren
mother and lover
shine in your beauty
songbird

Blessed be
on your sacred journey
May love's wings take you further
into the mystery
of life

Collective Consciousness

With a collective consciousness
turn your face to the sun
realise today
there is much to be done

The choice is yours
of how to respond
to each situation
you must go beyond

Walk in another's shoes
please be aware
if you live with abundance
then you have some to share

Don't move a mountain
just plant a seed
with love as your guide
you will soon see the need

Serendipity

The timeless dance of the veils
to shed footprints of attachment
and rebirth into a mystical union
resonates within

Immersed in surrender and gratitude
celestial pearls of wisdom
form rosaries of prayer
that entangle with my soul

Within this holy vibration
I come home to my heart

Now I shall open my wings
and fly

Sacred Self

As pure white light
draws you further into the mystery
may you remember seeker
you are connected
to the luminous essence
that you look for

May you always remember
the beloved
is your divine
and sacred self

Jewels of Insight

The only thing
that holds you back
from the source
is your thinking mind

Be still

The silent one awaits
to embellish you
with holy robes
and jewels of insight

Rite of Passage

Girl child I have watched you grow
into the woman I love and know
I bestow upon you blessings and love
may angels watch you from above

In your heart may you always hold dear
friends and loved ones
both far and near

May you always stand in your light
may you see the world as a glorious sight

Deep peace to you
as for the rest
may you always feel
forever blessed

Perfume of Love

The perfume of love
lingers
long after it has departed
being both my cure
and my pain

In this house of one
only the beloved remains
it is a holy fragrance
that I now seek

Invisible Grace

We dance upon the threshold
of another realm
catching glimpses of our
ethereal home

Upon our pilgrimage
gathering fragments of knowledge
we sew together
the threads of our fate

We have come here
still waiting to be born

Through invisible grace
life and death entwine

With the wings of our soul
wide open
we return safely home
to the light

Free Yourself

Shattered
my illusions
of control and familiarity
exhausted

I have cried an ocean
of frustrated tears
and I crumble
weeping and lost
to my knees

In complete surrender
I offer a prayer

Silence

Then
so quietly
almost like a breath
I sense a whisper

Let go child

Free yourself
and lose control

Earth School

Souls together on earth school
your sacred task
a precious jewel

Agreements made before your birth
your reasons here
to walk the earth

With divine purpose to everything
a sense of reverence
your journey will bring

Whispers of your heart and soul
will bring you closer
to your goal

In seeking love you will find
your inner voice
will gently remind
that what you search for
lays within
a sacred place
to begin

Fourth Generation

And you my girl child
you who seek more
than you see
you too have ink
running through your veins

You too look for light
where others may see darkness
scribing your visions
on parchment

You too are a lover
of paper and books
words and thoughts
a seeker of truth

This gift
is a blessing child
as you are
unto me

Meditation

Be still

Wrap yourself
in your robes of silence

Be drawn
into the mystery
of the absolute

Feel
your connection
to the whole

You are love

Law of Attraction

There is an ancient secret
that was hidden and suppressed
handed down among the elders
the truth's now manifest

It speaks of how to live your life
and be in harmony
with natural universal laws
as old as eternity

Keep your heart wide open
ask for what you desire
the universe will respond to you
blessings you will inspire

Allow your pure white light to shine
let it permeate
blessings waiting to be born
with reverence you create

Prayer

Revealing a holy shrine
night unfolds her robe of stars
gently across the heavens

Immersed
in this luminous essence
I give thanks
to the beloved

The intense pulse of prayer
permeates my soul
and enfolds me

In this state of utopia
knowing
I am wrapped up in love
I sleep

Omnipresent

You are divine
sacred
omnipresent

All that you are
connected
to all that there is

Blessed be
on your journey
of awakening

Divine Union

Now that I have found you
I said to the beloved
I am aware
of the distance between us

No
said the beloved
now that you have found me
you are a thousand miles closer
our souls are entangled
within this divine union

Immersed
in sacred love
we are one

Poison Arrows

Stand in your own light
don't give your strength away
words with poison arrows
don't listen to what they say

Stand in your own truth
don't take it all to heart
surround yourself with love
each moment a new start

Stand in your own strength
stand up brave and strong
let your warrior show herself
her teachings can't be wrong

Stand in your own grace
stand for love and peace
always try to do your best
your soul will find release

Faerie Emilie

On faerie wings and a prayer
she slips through the veil of illusion
returning safely home
to the primordial source

Her soul now free of earthly bonds
she writes a new page
in fate's book

Bathed in love and light
she is home again
within the rapture
of the beloved

Ancient Whispers

The echo
of ancient whispers
reach me
through the veil of time

Drawn gently into a mystical net
my sleeping memory awakens

Holy scriptures
intoxicate my soul

There in that bliss
infused in celestial knowledge
I feel my divine union
with truth

Divine Child

The birth
of a divine child
brings
the purest essence
of love
everlasting

Within the Darkness

Each moment
holds the sacred
if you choose to see
within both darkness
and the light
are gifts
for you and me

Learn to dance
in the rain
embrace
the raging storm
serenity
is yours to have
freewill
allows reform

Golden Thread

Just below
the surface of our lives
there is a golden thread
part of the weave
of all humanity

All souls are connected
to the needles
held within the hands
of the beloved
and woven gently
into creation

Infinite One

Around in circles
as if dancing on infinity's edge
my unknown longing
for the sacred mystery

My vision refused to see
deaf to the whispers
I did not understand
the infinite and I are one

Slowly
my eye opened
my memory awoke
I was in union
once again
as I had always been
with the primal source

The Beloved

You are the beloved
you and you alone
look inside your soul
see how much you've grown

You need not look outside of self
to know your hearts desires
all you need dwells within
your passion fuels the fires

Live in joy and harmony
follow all your dreams
the universe is waiting
nothing is as it seems

You are the beloved
when you realise this
you can surrender to your self
and live your life
in bliss

New Life

As the new year
unfurled her cloak of blessings
over the earth
a new life arrived

A girl child born
into cleansing waters
and enfolded
within the essence
of love

May your life be graced
with the holiness
of love and laughter

May you always feel the light
of your original source

Blessed be

I Am

I am a thousand winds that blow
I am the rain
I am the snow

I am the ocean
I am the earth
I am the infant
and woman in birth

I am the eagle
as she glides with grace
I am the smile
on my children's face

The essence of life
I am love
breathe me in
as below so above

Ask and You Shall Receive

I am eternally grateful
for what the universe provides
I would hardly dare believe it myself
but I have seen with my own eyes

All the dreams I dared to hold
are finally coming true
my heartfelt prayers are answered
but this I always knew

Blessings I have inspired
never doubting anything less
ask and you shall receive
such power we all possess

Never give up on your dreams
surrender as you go
gratitude holds the key
blessings it will bestow

Seekers of Light

Since the primordial birth of time
we are all seekers of light
though some may lose their way
caught up in mortal plight

We just need look within
to find our sacred fire
nothing can replace
no flesh or desire

No darkness will remain
when immersed in holy splendor
the magnificence of your being
makes it easy to surrender

Human Condition

Why is it
that the human condition
is to forever seek
that which we believe
to be outside of ourselves

To seek love
when it dwells within
to seek forgiveness
when it is by choice to forgive self
to pursue happiness
when it is already here

We choose not to see
that all along
we have always dwelled
not outside the essence
but within

Enter the threshold
of your beautiful self
for that mystical union you seek
is where love already abides

Awake and be Humble

Awake and be humble this new day
and know your mission here
children are dying mothers crying
no longer act from fear

Open your hearts and your minds
to the love they long to feel
they are no different to you or me
their misery is real

There is a difference you can make
you know it in your heart
listen as divine intervention
shows you where to start

Awaken to your calling
live in peace and love
this alone will spread to the world
carried on wings of a dove

Ecstasy

Deep within
the purity of your heart space
wrapped up gently in love and light
you can immerse yourself
in ecstasy

Allow yourself
to feel a sacred thread
your connection
to the original source

Here in this place
all souls resonate
within
a holy vibration

Wings Unfolded

On wings unfolded
into the light
your loved one
goes in peace

Memories
are yours to keep
may your soul
find some release

Walking Asleep

You have been walking asleep
within the eternal vastness

Awake now and be still

The soul of the universe
waits to enfold you
in pure white light

You are home

Spiritual Yearning

The day will dawn
when your arduous search
for a holy passion ends
in complete surrender
to self

As the veil parts
you clearly see
your hearts desire
has always been
a spiritual yearning

Awaken
at the sacred temple
of your own beautiful heart

The divine union
you seek
has always been within
waiting
for your embrace

Spirit Child

A child is born unto the earth
a gift from above
spiritually conceived
in celebration of your love

Enfold this child in robes of light
keep it safe from harm
this newborn soul before you now
will be your holy balm

A divine form of alchemy
has woven into being
the threads of fate and destiny
in human form now seen

Cloak of Indignation

It's a heavy fabric to wear
that cloak of indignation
woven from the threads
of injustice, greed and ignorance
you witness in this world

It may weigh heavily on your gentle soul
leaving its mark upon your shoulders

I offer to you a cloak
of healing, love and light
to wrap around yourself

Perhaps those of us
who choose to wear our cloaks of light
could join them together as one
wrapping them around
this beautiful planet
like a prayer

Universe Within a Universe

Mindfully walking
bare feet connected
to ancient earth
salty air
carrying my breath

Small tidal pools
sustaining aquatic entities
seemingly contained
within the mysterium
of their universe

Observer am I
the same aquatic roots
yet walking this earth
aware of my own
universe within a universe

Above me
sister moon and her union of stars
honoured guests
reflecting the infinite holy expansion
of something much bigger
than ourselves

Holding Space

Moments of light
still in gestation
tantalize and intrigue me

An old page turns
another
awaits to be born

Sensing hallowed ground
I place a bare foot
tentatively in front of me

Holding space
between the words
I invite you in

Peace Train

Journeying towards healing
we cannot walk as pilgrims
while carrying
the weight of the world
a personal crucifix
upon our shoulders

Disconnect and breathe
set down roots of peace
choose love and light
as soulfood

For love is a force
as real as gravity

Love will win

Book of Life

Our life stories
passages and volumes
scribed with memories
enfolded and bound within
a deep intimacy
of words

Narrating our stories
the threshold of change
brings new insight
memory
becomes fluid

Ripples of clarity
spill across ancient script
long forgotten passages
rewritten

Our book of life breathes
there is always another story
to be told

Memory is not scribed
in permanent ink

Bosom of the Earth

To the women who have raised me
raised me up picked me up loved me up
I bow to you

To those who have lost their way
found the way lit the way shown the way
I bow to you

To those who raise their children
raise other people's children make like a village
I bow to you

To those who stand naked in the holy wilderness of life
embracing all shadows of self
I bow to you

May all that is love
all that is grace
all that is sacred
unfold
as transformative balm
for your beautiful goddess hearts

Self Love

My feet imbibe as roots
on sacred land
hair tangled in stardust
moonlight
kisses my skin

Wild self dancing
betrothed to the holy one
an intimacy of breath
moves through me

Divine transformation
comes with surrender
back to grace

There is no freedom
without love

Disentangled

Falling deeper
into the mysteruim
paths of resistance surrender
as veils of dualism
disperse

Each soul seeded
to disentangle from form
dances to a mystical symphony
into the transformative womb
of the whole

Held by the holy other
our union sanctified
ancient pilgrims returning
into the vast holiness
of the absolute

Sacredness of Gestation

Moments of silence
body and soul healing
in the sacredness
of gestation

The illusion of the mind
constantly whispers for change
entertaining thoughts
of madness

A deep intimacy unfolds
integrating honoured guests
our shadow selves as one
trusting
everything is unfolding
in this holy flow

Remembering
to accept our vulnerability
seeing this ultimately
as our strength

Singing you Home

Singing you home
my creed is simple
my soul
a seeker of love

Resting within
a holy longing
for deep recognition
of another's
authenticity

I pray these words
carried on my breath
move through you
pouring light
into your soul

May your heart have wings

May you enter
where you already abide

Guardians

Earth guardians
storytellers of ancient times
honouring primordial roots
of sacred lands

Water guardians
protectors of the holy flow
deep within
the bosom of earth

Living for something bigger
than themselves
peacefully holding
sacred space

Gently reminding us
one life force connects
to the holy other

The Holy Making of the Day

Balm for my soul
small moments of grace
I open my heart to blessings
flowing through me

Aware of my essence
enfolding all parts of myself
shadow and light
into the sacred whole

I return inside to heal
breathing purpose and light
returning to innocence

This moment
impregnated with simply being
I surrender to love

The holy making of the day

For more about Earthschool Harmony
and her work please see:

Facebook: facebook.com/EarthschoolHarmony/
Instagram:
instagram.com/earthschool_harmony/
Twitter: twitter.com/earthschoolh

www.earthschoolharmony.com
earthschoolharmony@yahoo.com.au

You are welcome to write a book review online

Many thanks and Blessings